The Money Machine Blueprint: AI Edition"

Your Comprehensive Guide to Making Money Online through Artificial Intelligence

williams.koren

TABLE OF CONTENT

I. Introduction

II. Understanding the AI Landscape

III. Building Your Foundation

IV. Identifying Profitable AI Applications

Introduction:

Welcome to The Money Machine Blueprint: AI Edition

A. Welcome to the AI Revolution

In the fast-paced landscape of the digital era, we find ourselves standing at the crossroads of innovation and opportunity. Welcome to the AI Revolution, where the fusion of human ingenuity and artificial intelligence has opened doors to unprecedented possibilities. As we navigate this dynamic intersection, entrepreneurs like yourself have the chance to harness the power of AI and unlock new realms of online success. In this transformative journey, we embark on a quest to understand, implement, and thrive in the ever-evolving world of artificial intelligence.

B. The Promise of The Money Machine Blueprint

Imagine a world where your online ventures are not just lucrative but also powered by the cutting-edge intelligence of machines. Welcome to "The Money Machine Blueprint: AI Edition." This comprehensive guide is more than a book; it's your key to unraveling the potential of making money online through the strategic integration of artificial intelligence. The promise here is not merely financial gains, but a blueprint that equips you with the knowledge and tools to build a sustainable and thriving online business in the AI era. It's time to turn the gears of your very own money machine.

C. Setting Expectations for Readers

Before we delve into the depths of AI entrepreneurship, let's set clear expectations. This guide is designed for the curious, the ambitious, and those ready to seize the opportunities presented by AI. Whether you're a seasoned entrepreneur looking to diversify or someone starting their online journey, this blueprint caters to all. Expect a comprehensive exploration of AI fundamentals, practical insights on implementation, and a roadmap for monetizing AI solutions. The journey ahead will be both enlightening and rewarding, demanding your dedication and curiosity.

Get ready to witness the fusion of human potential and artificial intelligence, as we embark on a journey that promises not just financial prosperity but a paradigm shift in your approach to online business. Welcome to "The Money Machine Blueprint: AI Edition," where the future of online success begins.

CHAPTER 1: NAVIGATING THE AI LANDSCAPE

Embarking on a journey into the heart of the AI landscape, this chapter serves as our compass, guiding us through the intricacies of artificial intelligence and its profound impact on the world of online business.

A. Demystifying Artificial Intelligence in the Digital Age

In the digital age, the term "Artificial Intelligence" (AI) has transcended its status as a technological buzzword, emerging as a transformative force that shapes the way we interact with and perceive technology. At its essence, AI refers to the capability of machines to imitate intelligent human behavior. This section aims to demystify the complexities surrounding AI, offering a clear and accessible understanding of its components, functionalities, and applications in the contemporary digital landscape.

We'll delve into the diverse facets of AI, ranging from machine learning and natural language processing to computer vision. By comprehending these fundamental aspects, readers will gain a solid foundation to appreciate the role of AI in the broader context of online business and entrepreneurship.

B. Tracing the Arc of AI: Past, Present, and Future

Understanding the evolution of AI is paramount to grasping its current significance and anticipating its future potential. The journey begins with the theoretical foundations laid by pioneers like Alan Turing and the emergence of AI as an academic discipline. We'll navigate through the historical landscape, exploring the peaks and troughs of AI development, including the AI winters—periods of reduced funding and interest.

The present-day resurgence of AI is marked by groundbreaking advancements in computing power, the availability of vast datasets, and the refinement of complex algorithms. As we look to the future, we'll uncover the exciting prospects that lie ahead, from enhanced machine learning capabilities to the integration of AI into everyday aspects of our lives.

C. A Wave of Change: AI's Influence on Online Business Opportunities

The impact of AI on online business is comparable to a tidal wave, reshaping the landscape and offering new horizons for entrepreneurs. This section focuses on the tangible ways in which AI has become a game-changer for various sectors of online business, including e-commerce, content creation, and financial transactions.

By exploring real-world examples and case studies, readers will gain insights into how AI is not merely a technological advance but a catalyst for innovation. It opens doors to personalized customer experiences, data-driven decision-making, and the creation of new revenue streams. Entrepreneurs who understand and harness the power of AI position themselves at the forefront of the dynamic online marketplace.

This chapter is your gateway to a deeper understanding of AI and its implications for online business. Join me as we navigate this landscape, unraveling the potential it holds for those ready to embrace the future of entrepreneurship in the era of artificial intelligence.

CHAPTER 2:
BUILDING YOUR FOUNDATION

In the dynamic realm of artificial intelligence, establishing a robust foundation is essential for entrepreneurs looking to harness its power. This chapter serves as your guide to not only comprehend essential AI concepts but also navigate through the intricate jargon that often accompanies this transformative technology. Additionally, we'll delve into practical steps for setting up your digital workspace, ensuring a seamless journey towards AI success.

A. *Essential AI Concepts for Entrepreneurs*

To embark on a journey into the world of AI, it's crucial to grasp the fundamental concepts that underpin this technology. This section will break down these concepts in a digestible manner, catering specifically to entrepreneurs. We'll explore topics such as:

Machine Learning (ML): Understanding how machines learn from data and improve their performance over time.

Neural Networks: Unraveling the workings of artificial neural networks, the building blocks of deep learning.

Natural Language Processing (NLP): Navigating the technology that enables machines to understand, interpret, and generate human-like language.

Computer Vision: Exploring how machines can interpret and make decisions based on visual data, mimicking human vision.

By mastering these core concepts, entrepreneurs will gain a solid foundation to conceptualize and leverage AI in their ventures.

B. Navigating the AI Jargon: A Quick Glossary

The AI landscape is often adorned with a tapestry of technical terms and jargon that can be overwhelming. In this section, we'll provide a quick glossary, demystifying the terminology and acronyms that frequently populate discussions around AI. From "supervised learning" to "algorithmic bias," this glossary aims to empower entrepreneurs with the language necessary to engage in meaningful conversations about AI.

Understanding the jargon not only facilitates communication but also empowers entrepreneurs to make informed decisions regarding the integration of AI into their business strategies.

C. Setting Up Your Digital Workspace for AI Success

A critical aspect of leveraging AI is creating a conducive digital workspace that supports experimentation, development, and implementation. This section will guide entrepreneurs through the practical steps of setting up their digital workspace, covering:

Hardware and Software Requirements: Outlining the essential tools and technologies needed for AI endeavors.

Data Infrastructure: Addressing the importance of a robust infrastructure for handling and processing data.

Collaboration Tools: Exploring tools and platforms that facilitate collaboration among team members working on AI projects.

By the end of this section, entrepreneurs will be equipped with not only the knowledge of essential AI concepts but also the practical tools needed to lay the groundwork for AI success within their digital workspace.

This chapter aims to empower entrepreneurs with the knowledge and resources necessary to build a strong foundation in AI. As we navigate through the complexities, remember that your understanding of these concepts and tools will be the cornerstone of your success in the AI-driven digital landscape.

Chapter 3: Identifying Profitable AI Applications

As we continue our exploration into the realm of artificial intelligence, this chapter is dedicated to uncovering the diverse and profitable applications of AI. From revolutionizing e-commerce to reshaping content creation and enhancing financial insights, AI is a powerful tool that entrepreneurs can leverage to elevate their ventures.

A. AI in E-Commerce and Online Retail

In the dynamic world of e-commerce, AI has emerged as a game-changer, transforming the way businesses interact with customers and streamline operations. In this section, we'll delve into the specific applications of AI in e-commerce, including:

Personalized Recommendations: Discover how AI algorithms analyze user behavior to provide personalized product recommendations, enhancing the customer shopping experience.

Chatbots and Virtual Assistants: Explore the role of AI-powered chatbots and virtual assistants in improving customer support, answering queries, and facilitating seamless transactions.

Supply Chain Optimization: Understand how AI is utilized to optimize supply chain processes, from demand forecasting to inventory management.

By understanding and implementing these AI applications, entrepreneurs in the e-commerce space can gain a competitive edge and deliver enhanced value to their customers.

B. Content Creation and Marketing Strategies with AI

In the realm of digital content creation and marketing, AI introduces innovative solutions that redefine how businesses engage with their audience. This section will explore AI applications in content creation, marketing strategies, and beyond:

Automated Content Generation: Learn how AI-powered tools can assist in creating engaging and relevant content, from articles and blog posts to social media updates.

Targeted Marketing Campaigns: Discover the potential of AI in analyzing consumer data to create highly targeted and personalized marketing campaigns.

Predictive Analytics: Understand how AI algorithms can predict trends and consumer behavior, allowing entrepreneurs to make data-driven decisions in their marketing efforts.

Entrepreneurs who harness the power of AI in content creation and marketing stand to unlock new levels of efficiency and effectiveness in reaching their target audience.

C. Financial Insights: Investing and Wealth Management

AI's influence extends into the financial realm, offering insights and opportunities for investors and wealth managers. In this section, we'll explore how AI is reshaping financial landscapes, covering:

Algorithmic Trading: Examine how AI algorithms analyze market trends and execute trades at speeds unattainable by human traders.

Personalized Financial Advice: Learn how AI-driven platforms provide personalized financial advice based on individual goals and risk profiles.

Fraud Detection and Security: Understand the role of AI in enhancing financial security by detecting fraudulent activities and safeguarding sensitive information.

Entrepreneurs involved in finance and investing can benefit significantly from integrating AI into their strategies, gaining a competitive advantage and providing enhanced services to clients.

This chapter is designed to guide entrepreneurs in identifying and understanding profitable AI applications within specific industries. By exploring the transformative potential of AI in e-commerce, content creation, and financial insights, you'll be better equipped to leverage this technology to propel your ventures into the future.

CHAPTER 4:
DEVELOPING YOUR AI SKILLSET

In the fast-evolving landscape of AI-driven entrepreneurship, acquiring and honing relevant skills is paramount. This chapter is dedicated to helping you build a robust AI skillset, providing essential guidance, learning resources, and real-world examples of successful skill development.

A. Essential Skills for AI-Driven Entrepreneurship

Navigating the intersection of AI and entrepreneurship requires a unique set of skills. In this section, we'll explore the essential skills necessary for success in AI-driven ventures:

Data Literacy: Understand the fundamentals of data, including collection, analysis, and interpretation—a foundational skill for AI entrepreneurs.

Programming Proficiency: Gain insights into programming languages like Python and frameworks such as TensorFlow or PyTorch, crucial for implementing AI solutions.

Machine Learning Expertise: Develop a comprehensive understanding of machine learning concepts, algorithms, and techniques that form the backbone of AI applications.

Critical Thinking and Problem-Solving: Cultivate the ability to approach challenges analytically, identifying opportunities for AI integration and problem-solving.

Business Acumen: Combine technical knowledge with a keen understanding of business dynamics to effectively implement AI strategies aligned with organizational goals.

By honing these skills, aspiring AI entrepreneurs can establish a solid foundation for success in the rapidly evolving AI landscape.

B. Learning Resources and Strategies for Skill Acquisition

Embarking on the journey to acquire AI skills requires effective learning resources and strategies. This section provides guidance on where and how to acquire these skills:

Online Courses and Platforms: Explore reputable online platforms and courses specializing in AI, such as Coursera, edX, and Udacity.

Books and Publications: Delve into recommended books and publications that cover AI fundamentals, best practices, and emerging trends.

Hands-On Projects: Embrace a hands-on approach by engaging in real-world projects to reinforce theoretical knowledge and gain practical experience.

Industry Certifications: Consider pursuing industry-recognized certifications to validate your AI skills and enhance your credibility in the field.

Networking and Community Engagement: Join AI communities, attend conferences, and participate in networking events to connect with experts and fellow learners, fostering a collaborative learning environment.

By strategically leveraging these resources and approaches, entrepreneurs can efficiently build and expand their AI skillset.

C. Real-world Examples of Successful AI Skill Development

Inspiration often stems from real-world success stories. In this section, we'll delve into examples of entrepreneurs who have successfully developed their AI skillsets:

Entrepreneurial AI Pioneers: Explore the stories of entrepreneurs who have seamlessly integrated AI into their ventures, reshaping industries and achieving remarkable success.

Learning from Failures: Understand the challenges faced by entrepreneurs on their AI learning journeys and learn valuable lessons from their failures.

Adaptability and Continuous Learning: Witness how successful AI entrepreneurs embrace a mindset of adaptability and continuous learning, staying ahead of the curve.

These real-world examples serve as beacons of inspiration, demonstrating that with dedication and strategic skill development, anyone can become proficient in AI-driven entrepreneurship.

This chapter aims to guide you through the process of developing a strong AI skillset. By understanding the essential skills, exploring effective learning resources, and drawing inspiration from real-world successes, you'll be better equipped to navigate the exciting and ever-changing landscape of AI-driven entrepreneurship.

Chapter 5: Implementing AI in Your Online Ventures

As we delve deeper into the application of artificial intelligence (AI) in the entrepreneurial landscape, this chapter is dedicated to the practical aspects of implementation. We'll explore how entrepreneurs can seamlessly integrate AI into their online ventures, maximizing its potential in e-commerce, content optimization, and financial decision-making.

A. Integrating AI into E-Commerce Platforms

E-commerce has become a cornerstone of online entrepreneurship, and AI is transforming how businesses engage with customers and streamline operations. In this section, we'll focus on the integration of AI into e-commerce platforms, covering key strategies such as:

Personalized Customer Experiences: Explore how AI algorithms can analyze customer behavior and preferences to deliver personalized recommendations and experiences.

Dynamic Pricing Strategies: Understand how AI can be utilized for dynamic pricing, optimizing product prices based on market conditions, demand, and competitor pricing.

Chatbots and Virtual Assistants: Implement AI-driven chatbots and virtual assistants to enhance customer support, providing instant assistance and improving overall user satisfaction.

By seamlessly integrating AI into e-commerce platforms, entrepreneurs can create a more personalized and efficient shopping experience for their customers.

B. Maximizing AI for Content Optimization and Marketing

In the realm of digital content and marketing, AI introduces innovative solutions to optimize strategies and engage audiences effectively. This section will explore how entrepreneurs can leverage AI for content creation, marketing, and beyond:

Automated Content Creation: Learn how AI tools can assist in generating high-quality, relevant content for various platforms, saving time and resources.

Targeted Marketing Campaigns: Understand the power of AI in analyzing customer data to create highly targeted and personalized marketing campaigns, increasing engagement and conversion rates.

Predictive Analytics: Explore how AI-driven predictive analytics can forecast trends and consumer behavior, enabling entrepreneurs to make data-driven decisions in their marketing efforts.

By maximizing AI for content optimization and marketing, entrepreneurs can stay ahead of the curve, delivering compelling content to their target audience and driving business growth.

C. Leveraging AI Tools for Financial Analysis and Decision-Making

Financial analysis and decision-making are critical components of entrepreneurial success. In this section, we'll focus on leveraging AI tools for financial insights, covering key areas such as:

Algorithmic Trading: Explore how AI algorithms can analyze market trends and execute trades at speeds unattainable by human traders, optimizing investment portfolios.

Personalized Financial Advice: Understand how AI-driven platforms provide personalized financial advice based on individual goals and risk profiles, enhancing the client experience in wealth management.

Fraud Detection and Security: Implement AI tools for detecting fraudulent activities, safeguarding financial transactions, and ensuring the security of sensitive information.

By incorporating AI into financial analysis and decision-making, entrepreneurs can make informed, data-driven choices that contribute to the overall success and stability of their ventures.

This chapter serves as a practical guide for entrepreneurs looking to implement AI in their online ventures. By exploring real-world applications in e-commerce, content optimization, and financial decision-making, you'll gain insights into how AI can be a transformative force in enhancing various aspects of your business.

CHAPTER 6:
MONETIZING AI SOLUTIONS

In this pivotal chapter, we shift our focus from implementation to monetization, exploring the diverse avenues through which entrepreneurs can profit from their AI endeavors. From creating and selling AI products to crafting a sustainable business model, we'll delve into the strategies that have proven successful for entrepreneurs venturing into the lucrative field of artificial intelligence.

A. Creating and Selling AI Products and Services

Creating and selling AI products and services is a dynamic avenue for entrepreneurial success. In this section, we'll explore strategies for entrepreneurs looking to turn their AI innovations into marketable products and services:

Identifying Market Needs: Understand how entrepreneurs can identify gaps in the market and leverage AI to create solutions that meet specific needs.

Product Development Strategies: Explore the process of developing AI products, including the importance of user feedback, iterative improvements, and staying abreast of technological advancements.

Service Offerings: Learn how entrepreneurs can provide AI-related services, such as consulting, implementation, and ongoing support to businesses looking to adopt AI solutions.

By effectively creating and selling AI products and services, entrepreneurs can tap into a growing market hungry for innovative solutions.

B. Crafting Your AI Business Model

Crafting a robust business model is essential for the long-term success of AI-driven ventures. This section will guide entrepreneurs through the process of developing a sustainable business model for their AI endeavors:

Revenue Streams: Explore various revenue streams associated with AI, including product sales, subscription models, licensing, and service-based income.

Cost Structure: Understand the costs associated with AI development, deployment, and maintenance, ensuring a clear understanding of financial implications.

Value Proposition: Define the unique value proposition that your AI solutions bring to the market, differentiating your business from competitors.

Crafting a solid business model ensures that entrepreneurs not only create valuable AI solutions but also establish a foundation for financial viability and growth.

C. Case Studies: Successful Entrepreneurs Profiting from AI

Real-world examples provide invaluable insights into the practical application of strategies. In this section, we'll delve into case studies of successful entrepreneurs who have navigated the complex landscape of monetizing AI solutions:

AI in Healthcare: Explore how entrepreneurs have capitalized on AI to revolutionize healthcare, from diagnostic tools to personalized treatment plans.

E-Commerce Optimization: Learn from businesses that have leveraged AI to enhance customer experiences, increase sales, and streamline operations in the e-commerce sector.

Financial Technology (Fintech): Discover how entrepreneurs in fintech have used AI to innovate in areas such as algorithmic trading, robo-advisors, and fraud detection.

By examining these case studies, entrepreneurs can glean practical insights, inspiration, and strategic considerations for monetizing their own AI solutions.

This chapter serves as a comprehensive guide for entrepreneurs looking to turn their AI initiatives into profitable ventures. By exploring the creation and sale of AI products, developing sustainable business models, and drawing inspiration from successful case studies, you'll be well-equipped to navigate the intricacies of monetizing AI solutions.

Chapter 7:
Overcoming Challenges and Pitfalls

As we navigate the promising landscape of AI entrepreneurship, it is imperative to address the challenges and pitfalls that entrepreneurs may encounter. This chapter delves into dispelling common myths, navigating ethical considerations, and overcoming technical challenges associated with AI ventures.

A. Common Myths and Misconceptions About AI

In the realm of AI entrepreneurship, several myths and misconceptions can hinder progress. This section aims to debunk these myths, offering clarity to entrepreneurs:

AI as a Panacea: Dispel the myth that AI is a one-size-fits-all solution and emphasize the importance of understanding its limitations.

Fear of Job Displacement: Address concerns about AI leading to widespread job loss by highlighting the potential for job creation and augmentation.

Perception of Complexity: Clarify misconceptions regarding the complexity of AI, making it accessible and understandable for entrepreneurs at all levels.

By dispelling these myths, entrepreneurs can approach AI with a realistic and informed mindset, unlocking its true potential.

B. Ethical Considerations in AI Entrepreneurship

As AI becomes an integral part of entrepreneurship, ethical considerations take center stage. This section explores the ethical dimensions associated with AI ventures:

Bias and Fairness: Address the challenge of bias in AI algorithms and strategies to ensure fairness and inclusivity.

Transparency and Accountability: Emphasize the importance of transparency in AI decision-making processes and the accountability of entrepreneurs for the ethical implications of their AI solutions.

Privacy Concerns: Navigate the delicate balance between leveraging user data for AI insights and respecting privacy rights.

By proactively addressing ethical considerations, entrepreneurs can build trustworthy AI solutions that align with societal values and expectations.

C. Technical Challenges and How to Navigate Them

The technical landscape of AI entrepreneurship is not without hurdles.

This section explores common technical challenges and offers guidance on overcoming them:

Data Quality and Availability: Address issues related to the quality and availability of data, emphasizing strategies for data collection, cleaning, and augmentation.

Algorithmic Complexity: Navigate the complexity of AI algorithms by advocating for a gradual learning approach and providing resources for algorithmic understanding.

Integration with Existing Systems: Guide entrepreneurs on integrating AI solutions seamlessly with their existing technological infrastructure, avoiding disruptions.

By providing practical insights into overcoming these technical challenges, entrepreneurs can approach AI implementation with confidence and resilience.

This chapter serves as a roadmap for entrepreneurs to navigate and overcome challenges associated with AI entrepreneurship. By dispelling myths, addressing ethical considerations, and providing solutions to technical challenges, entrepreneurs can forge a path towards successful and responsible AI ventures.

Chapter 8:
Future Trends and Opportunities

As we look towards the future of AI in the entrepreneurial landscape, this chapter explores emerging trends, strategies for positioning oneself amidst innovations, and long-term approaches to sustain AI-driven income. By staying ahead of the curve, entrepreneurs can capitalize on the dynamic opportunities that the future holds.

A. Emerging Trends in AI and Online Business

The landscape of AI and online business is ever-evolving. In this section, we'll delve into the emerging trends that are likely to shape the future:

Explainable AI (XAI): Explore the rising demand for AI systems that provide transparent and understandable explanations for their decision-making processes.

AI-powered Cybersecurity: Examine the increasing role of AI in fortifying online security, identifying threats, and implementing proactive measures against cyber-attacks.

Edge Computing and AI: Understand how the integration of AI with edge computing is becoming pivotal, enabling faster processing and real-time decision-making in distributed systems.

By staying informed about these emerging trends, entrepreneurs can position themselves to capitalize on new opportunities and remain at the forefront of AI innovation.

B. Positioning Yourself for Future AI Innovations

Anticipating and preparing for future AI innovations is a key aspect of sustained success. This section provides strategies for entrepreneurs to position themselves effectively:

Continuous Learning: Emphasize the importance of staying updated on AI advancements through continuous learning, attending conferences, and participating in industry forums.

Networking and Collaboration: Advocate for building a strong network within the AI community, fostering collaborations that can lead to mutual growth and exploration of new opportunities.

Agile Adaptation: Encourage an agile mindset, where entrepreneurs can quickly adapt to new technologies and trends, ensuring they are well-prepared for future disruptions.

By adopting these strategies, entrepreneurs can position themselves as innovators and thought leaders in the evolving landscape of AI entrepreneurship.

C. Long-Term Strategies for Sustainable AI-Driven Income

Sustainable income from AI ventures requires a long-term perspective. This section explores strategies for ensuring ongoing success:

Diversification of AI Solutions: Encourage entrepreneurs to diversify their AI offerings, catering to various industries and adapting their solutions to changing market needs.

Investment in Research and Development: Stress the importance of dedicating resources to ongoing research and development, ensuring that AI solutions remain cutting-edge and competitive.

Ethical and Responsible AI: Highlight the significance of embedding ethical considerations into AI solutions, fostering trust among users and ensuring long-term sustainability.

By implementing these long-term strategies, entrepreneurs can build a resilient foundation for sustainable income in the dynamic and evolving AI landscape.

This chapter serves as a guide to entrepreneurs looking to navigate the future of AI and online business. By understanding emerging trends, positioning oneself for innovations, and adopting long-term strategies, entrepreneurs can seize the opportunities that lie ahead and ensure continued success in the world of AI-driven entrepreneurship.

CHAPTER 9:
RESOURCES AND TOOLS

In this chapter, we'll explore a curated list of resources and tools that will empower AI entrepreneurs on their journey. From essential AI tools and platforms to vibrant online communities and further reading materials, these resources aim to provide a comprehensive toolkit for entrepreneurs seeking to thrive in the dynamic field of artificial intelligence.

A. Recommended AI Tools and Platforms

TensorFlow: An open-source machine learning framework developed by Google, TensorFlow is widely used for building and training machine learning models.

PyTorch: Another popular open-source deep learning framework, PyTorch is known for its flexibility and dynamic computational graph, making it a favorite among researchers and developers.

IBM Watson: IBM's AI platform offers a range of services, including machine learning, natural language processing, and computer vision, providing comprehensive AI capabilities.

Microsoft Azure AI: Azure AI provides a suite of tools and services for building AI solutions, from pre-built models to custom machine learning models.

Google Cloud AI Platform: Google Cloud offers a range of AI and machine learning services, enabling developers to build, train, and deploy models on the cloud.

By leveraging these tools and platforms, entrepreneurs can accelerate their AI development processes and create sophisticated solutions for their ventures.

B. Online Communities for AI Entrepreneurs

Kaggle: A vibrant platform for data science and machine learning enthusiasts, Kaggle provides a collaborative environment for competitions, discussions, and shared resources.

AI Entrepreneurship Forums: Explore online forums dedicated to AI entrepreneurship, such as the AI section on Reddit or specialized AI entrepreneur communities, fostering networking and knowledge-sharing.

LinkedIn Groups: Join relevant LinkedIn groups focused on AI entrepreneurship, where professionals share insights, job opportunities, and engage in discussions.

AI Meetup Groups: Attend local or virtual AI meetup groups to connect with like-minded entrepreneurs, researchers, and professionals in your region.

By actively participating in these communities, entrepreneurs can tap into a wealth of knowledge, build valuable connections, and stay updated on the latest trends in AI.

C. Further Reading and Learning Materials

Books:

"Artificial Intelligence: A Guide for Thinking Humans" by Melanie Mitchell.
"Life 3.0: Being Human in the Age of Artificial Intelligence" by Max Tegmark.
"Machine Learning Yearning" by Andrew Ng.

Online Courses:

"AI for Everyone" on Coursera by Andrew Ng.
"Deep Learning Specialization" on Coursera by Andrew Ng.
"AI and Machine Learning for Business" on edX by Columbia University.
Research Papers:

Explore research papers on platforms like arXiv.org to delve into the latest advancements in AI and related fields.
Blogs and News Outlets:

Follow reputable AI blogs and news outlets, such as Towards Data Science, Synced, and The AI Report, for timely updates and insights.

By immersing themselves in these learning materials, entrepreneurs can deepen their understanding of AI concepts, stay informed about industry developments, and continuously enhance their skills.

This chapter serves as a comprehensive guide to the valuable resources and tools available for AI entrepreneurs. By utilizing these assets, entrepreneurs can equip themselves with the knowledge, skills, and community support needed to navigate the intricate and ever-evolving landscape of artificial intelligence.

CHAPTER 10: CONCLUSION

In this final chapter, we bring our journey through "The Money Machine Blueprint: AI Edition" to a close. As we reflect on the insights gained, opportunities uncovered, and challenges addressed, this conclusion serves to encapsulate the essence of the blueprint, offer encouragement for aspiring AI entrepreneurs, and share closing thoughts on the future of AI in the realm of online money-making.

A. Summing Up The Money Machine Blueprint

"The Money Machine Blueprint" has been a comprehensive guide, unveiling the potential of AI as a transformative force in online entrepreneurship. We've explored the essential concepts, navigated challenges, and charted a course for integrating AI into various facets of online ventures. As we bring this blueprint to a close, let's revisit the core principles that form its foundation:

Understanding AI Concepts: We demystified the world of artificial intelligence, providing entrepreneurs with the knowledge to harness its power.

Building a Strong Foundation: From essential skills to setting up a digital workspace, we laid the groundwork for successful AI-driven ventures.

Identifying Profitable Applications: We delved into specific sectors, showcasing how AI can revolutionize e-commerce, content creation, and financial insights.

Implementing AI Solutions:
Entrepreneurs learned to integrate AI seamlessly into their ventures, from e-commerce platforms to content optimization and financial decision-making.

Monetizing AI Solutions: The blueprint guided entrepreneurs in turning their AI initiatives into profitable endeavors, crafting business models that ensure long-term success.

Overcoming Challenges: We addressed common myths, ethical considerations, and technical challenges, providing insights to navigate these hurdles effectively.

Future Trends and Opportunities: Entrepreneurs gained a forward-looking perspective, exploring emerging trends, strategies for innovation, and long-term approaches to sustain AI-driven income.

Resources and Tools: The chapter provided a curated set of resources, tools, and communities to empower entrepreneurs on their AI journey.

B. Encouragement for Readers to Dive into AI Entrepreneurship

To the readers who have embarked on this journey, I extend heartfelt encouragement.

AI entrepreneurship is a dynamic and rewarding path, and your willingness to explore this frontier is commendable. As you step into the world of AI, remember:

Continuous Learning: AI is an ever-evolving field. Embrace a mindset of continuous learning to stay at the forefront of innovation.

Resilience in Challenges: Challenges are inherent in any entrepreneurial journey. Approach them with resilience, viewing them as opportunities for growth.

Community Engagement: Connect with fellow AI enthusiasts, entrepreneurs, and experts. Communities offer support, collaboration, and diverse perspectives.

Ethical Considerations: As you innovate, prioritize ethical considerations. Building trustworthy and responsible AI solutions contributes to long-term success.

Innovation and Adaptability: The future belongs to those who innovate and adapt. Stay curious, experiment with new ideas, and be agile in response to changing trends.

C. Closing Thoughts on the Future of AI in Online Money-Making

As we conclude this blueprint, let's reflect on the future of AI in the landscape of online money-making. The fusion of AI and entrepreneurship is an exciting frontier, promising limitless possibilities. In the years to come:

Evolving Opportunities: AI will continue to unlock new opportunities in diverse industries, reshaping how entrepreneurs approach online ventures.

Human-AI Collaboration: The synergy between human creativity and AI capabilities will become increasingly pronounced, leading to unprecedented innovations.

Ethical and Responsible AI: Society's demand for ethical and responsible AI solutions will shape the industry, emphasizing the importance of transparency and fairness.

Entrepreneurial Leadership:
Entrepreneurs who embrace AI, lead with purpose, and address societal needs will play a pivotal role in shaping the future landscape.

In the grand tapestry of AI entrepreneurship, each entrepreneur contributes a unique thread. As you forge ahead, envision the impact you can make, the solutions you can create, and the future you can shape. The Money Machine Blueprint has equipped you with the tools; now, it's your turn to paint the canvas of AI entrepreneurship with your vision and ingenuity.

To every reader who embarked on this journey, I extend my best wishes. May your AI ventures be marked by innovation, resilience, and sustained success. As the curtain falls on this blueprint, a new chapter begins for you, the AI entrepreneur of tomorrow. Best of luck on your endeavors, and may the future be rich with the rewards of your entrepreneurial spirit.